To Linda

How to Stop Brand Stealing Thieves

Your Brand Protection Playbook

LETONYA F. MOORE

I'm honored to now be in your network! *signature*

How to Stop Brand Stealing Thieves : Your Brand Protection
Playbook

For information contact www.iprotectyourbrand.com

Book and Cover design by SDAP Marketing

ISBN: 978-1-734-0117-0-8

First Edition: September 2019

Contents

INTRODUCTION

NOTE: NOTHING CONTAINED HEREIN IS TO BE CONSTRUED AS LEGAL ADVICE OR TO CREATE AN ATTORNEY-CLIENT RELATIONSHIP. PLEASE SEEK COUNSEL BEFORE MAKING ANY BUSINESS OR PERSONAL DECISIONS.

A lot of people have dreams and aspirations of having their own businesses; but are crippled by the fear of someone stealing their ideas or taking their money for services they do not need. In my practice, I have potential clients who contact me because someone has taken advantage of them or someone has imitated their brand to the point of dilution or they have stolen their logo. Those are the "easy" situations and we resolve those quickly. The more difficult situation is the business owner with a dream that has been dashed because they failed to understand the importance of having the right systems in place to keep it safe. The purpose of this book is to educate you about the essential elements you need to protect your business, inform you of exactly the steps to take, and give you the blueprint for making sure you are protected.

My sole objective is to provide insight and guidance to those seeking to be in the best possible position to protect their brand from the outset. It is my hope that you can take what you learn in this book and get in the power seat of your brand, equipped with knowledge necessary to keep brand snatchers at bay.

What you will discover are the introductory steps to protecting your brand and establishing the foundation to make business growth attainable. In the coming chapters you will learn how to be prepared and to be protected. You will learn the right questions to ask the essential B.A.I.L. members of your team (I'll explain the B.A.I.L. team in subsequent chapters) before you bring them aboard. You will learn the "true" value of intellectual property and how to distinguish a copyright from a trademark, and know which one you will need. Most importantly, you will learn how to successfully barter and collaborate with other brands to help your brand grow exponentially. At the end of the book, there is a glossary of terms to better define common terms used in this book. In addition, there is a companion workbook and sample agreements available to assist you with your brand protection journey.

Now, let us strategize for success!

1

Be Prepared...Be Protected
How to Stop Collaborators from Stealing Your Idea

One major area of concern for clients is how to stop collaborators from stealing ideas and doing it themselves. In this chapter, you will learn some practical components of brand protection, how you may unwittingly open the door to a brand thief, tools to protect your intellectual property and how to effectively prepare for the collaboration.

Brand protection has both an internal and an external component. Oftentimes, entrepreneurs fail to consider their collaborators, staff, or even that friend that you talk with about your great idea, and how this conversation opens the door for the brand thief. When you get that magnificent idea or the dose of inspiration, keep it to yourself. The very first commitment you need to make in this brand protection journey is to change your mindset. How you treat your ideas are a direct reflection of how you value yourself. The first line of defense is to understand that you are worthy and valuable, your ideas and creations are valuable and profitable.

Ask yourself, "If I hit the lottery, would I immediately tell the world?" For most of you, the answer is a quick and fast no. Then why would you tell the world about what could be the most profitable thing you have ever created? Before you even consider collaboration, you need the proper tools to protect your intellectual property in place. In the words of the great, Dr. Myles Munroe, "write this down". The tools include the following:

- understanding whether you need collaborators, service providers or experts;
- how to properly vet the potential collaborator, service provider or expert; and
- what type of agreements to have in place to secure your information before, during, and after the project.

HOW TO STOP BRAND STEALING THIEVES

First, let us take a look at some common scenarios. You have this *freaking fascinating* idea and you want to share it with people that you believe will be instrumental in making the vision a reality. You think, "So and so would be great to be on the team. I am going to reach out to them and I am going to tell them this idea that we can do together." You bring in someone to help "realize the vision" or "implement the program", only to look up later and see them implementing it without you.

Do not be ashamed or angry because we all have been there, whether we admit it or not. Another situation is when one person has an idea sparked and just are not sure what to do to get it moving. They bring in other people to help them really flesh out that idea, this is called the brainstorm team. For purposes of this discussion, note that an idea is not ripe for ownership until it becomes tangible.

When you gather your brainstorm team, you have created a collaborative and the final project can be construed as a result of   multiple   efforts,   ideas,   and   input.

Answer this question *are your brainstorm team members entitled to share in the ownership or profits of the final project?*

Keep in mind that you have brought them together specifically to assist you with taking your idea from concept to fruition. The answer is, it depends. Here's the play to making that determination:

- Did you have an agreement?
- What does your agreement call for?
- What terms did you put in place before engaging in the brainstorm session?
- Did you verbally discuss how ownership is going to be distributed before getting started?

For most of you, the answer is going to be no to all questions. These are the questions you must answer before engaging with your brainstorm team members. The companion workbook will help you map out the answers and get focused.

One of the top reasons there are problems at this stage is because you really did not understand or appreciate the value of your idea. How do I know this? I know this because people that understand the value of something will take the necessary steps to provide protection for it, like enlisting expert advice. Remember the lottery question? Generally when someone knows they are coming into a large sum of money, they think about who can assist them with making it grow and protect it. This person is almost never a friend or family member.

However, with their ideas, most people avoid contacting a lawyer or other professional because they are afraid of the cost, or getting taken advantage of, or just not being sure that it is worth it. In the world of "do it yourself " (DIY) everything, it's become commonplace for people to attempt to do things themselves and more often than not it creates an even bigger problem. Engage experts very early in the process. Why? Sharing it with an expert or consultant is not the same as engaging with a collaborator.

The right person with the right expertise is able to bring to the physical world, what was in your brain. This is your creation. Here is the caveat, professionals like engineers, chemists, architect and the like, are fee for service providers. Fee for service providers are persons with a particular skill set that provide a service for a small fee. They get paid to produce what you have asked them to produce. When enlisting services from this type of provider make sure that you have a fee for service agreement that reserves full intellectual property ownership to you. This connection is not a friendship but is a business relationship.

Having a relationship with the right expert is critical to protecting your brand. Although sharing information with experts is different from sharing information with collaborators, you want to make sure that you have a non-disclosure agreement (or clause) and in addition to the fee for services contract in place. Refer to the sample fee for service agreement in the *Brand Protection Toolkit.*

Later in this playbook, you will find the steps to having a guided conversation with potential experts and service providers to determine if they are a good fit for your brand. Most people skip the experts and they start seeking support for individuals in their circles. This can be extremely detrimental if you are not prepared and a common scenario that results in their intellectual property being stolen or usurped.

Ideas are like currency. Would you hand your money over to any other person without properly vetting them? When you start sharing ideas and having brainstorm sessions or openly sharing information haphazardly, that is essentially what you are doing. In chapter 4, how to handle the collaboration relationship will be discussed n detail, but for now, understand that when you enlist collaborators without establishing the terms you are essentially giving away currency. Collaboration means all parties are going to be providing input, ideas, and possibly sweat equity. We have seen it happen where either someone drops the ball or someone decides, "well I do not need him or her"…and then it happens. They push forward on their own but they take the information that they've learned from you and they capitalize on it.

This is why being proactive is critical.

Here's the play before you engage the brainstorm team, follow these steps:

- Determine the professionals/partners/resources you need not by name but by function.
- Determine why you need them.
- Think critically about the information you are proposing to share with that particular person.
- Have your agreements ready for signature before moving forward.

You can find the full exercise in the *How to Stop Brand Stealing Thieves Workbook.*

When assembling your brainstorm team, have them sign a non-disclosure agreement with a non-compete clause. In essence, you are protecting yourself from unlawful disclosure and preventing them from competing in the same market with the same or similar idea. Later in this book we will discuss more on non-compete/disclosure clauses and other agreements mentioned in this chapter.

When you develop an idea, always determine whether this is something you wish to explore, exploit (in the good sense) and expound upon. If the answer is yes, before you make your awesome idea known to the public, you must protect it. Oh...did I say, protect it? I'll discuss those exact steps later in this book.

I must be realistic with you, there are some situations where people are just not going to sign anything before you talk to them. If you find yourself in that situation, then you have a decision to make. Is **this one person** so valuable to your project that you risk them not signing the non-disclosure agreement? If the answer is yes, it is imperative that you conduct thorough due diligence research and consult with an attorney before any disclosures are made.

In addition to the brainstorm team, some people work with a think tank or mastermind group. If you find yourself in need of a "think tank" then make sure they have some skin in the game. Your think tank is your top-level squad that comes to the table bringing a necessary success component. A necessary success component is an element that is so ingrained in the success of the project that by not having it the project cannot succeed. The mastermind group, as described by Napoleon Hill in his writings, is a group of two or more people coming together in harmony to solve problems. Mastermind groups tend to have built in protections because generally the leader of the mastermind group has created a contract that covers areas like confidentiality, conflicts of interest, non-disclosure and competition, among other factors that could undermine the credibility and success of the group. If you are enlisting the assistance of a mastermind group, you want to make sure that the agreement fully protects your brand.

A critical part of your analysis is to make the distinction between each, service provider, collaborator, mastermind, and the think tank. Use the tools that you have learned in this chapter and conduct the analysis.

Remember the foundational principles:

- Do your due diligence upfront;
- Know your audience;
- Understand what is critical to success;
- Know your vital team members; and
- Create the list.

Here is a success strategy for navigating the collaboration conversation: The *"3 Rules to Navigating the Collaboration Conversation".*

- Rule Number 1: Tell them what, without telling them how. There is a method of how to explain what you are doing without giving away the gold. The goal is to leave the room where people are excited about your venture, but they do not have so much information that they can take that information and do it themselves. If you are presenting to potential collaborative partners or investors, they more than likely have other resources to realize the vision.

- Rule Number 2: Have the proper written agreements in place. If you proceed without a signed agreement, you are potentially putting your business or project at risk. *Refer to the samples in the Brand Protection Toolkit.*

- Rule Number 3: Ease the concern. When someone is apprehensive about signing an agreement, it does not always mean they are looking to do dirt. Sometimes, they are just concerned about not understanding what they are signing.

Here's the Play: "I am going to be sharing non-public, proprietary information with you and I have a duty to protect that information. Signing this non-disclosure is our formal agreement that you will not take our non-public, proprietary information and share it with anyone else without a need to know." If after you take the time to explain the situation, they still refuse to sign the non-disclosure, it is certainly a **red flag.**

Here's the Play when securing the non-disclosure agreement:

- Rule Number 1: Do not solely rely on an agreement from an online database. Now for those of you that know, I am NOT a proponent of getting anything offline...period. The best way is to connect with someone who can provide the service for you, or consult your *Brand Protection Toolkit* for a sample.

- Rule Number 2: Make sure that you file the executed copies in a safe place where you can get access to them at any time. Be sure to give the signatory a copy of the executed agreement and record that they received in with a confirmation email.

Following these simple rules before you start to pitch, can save you hundreds of dollars and can also save you thousands down the road. Do not let the fact that you may not have money to do all this at once, cause you to make decisions out of desperation. Follow the steps to implement success.

-#BRANDPROTECTIONTIP

Have consultants and independent contractors sign appropriate Confidentiality and Invention Assignment Agreements

-THE GLOBAL BRAND PROTECTOR

WWW.IPROTECTYOURBRAND.COM

2

HAVE THE B.A.I.L. READY?

Many business owners fail to assemble the right team of professionals to ensure their success. I call this the BAIL Team: Banker, Accountant, Insurance Professional and Lawyer. Why the BAIL Team? Because this is the team you need to get you out of any sticky situation in which you may find yourself.

BANKER

Your bank is not just a place where you put your money, get loans or leverage credit. Building a true banking relationship can prove to be one of the most powerful relationships you need in your business. For small business owners, access to capital is consistently listed among the top challenges.

HOW TO STOP BRAND STEALING THIEVES

Creating a banking partnership can ease or even alleviate that problem, but there are more advantages to the relationship than access to cash, especially if the bank specializes in helping small business owners grow.

Banks that specialize in assisting small businesses can assist with immediate business needs and help you make future financial plans. So why do not more small business owners have relationships with the bank? It is simple; most believe that this level is reserved for larger businesses and corporations. Inc.com provides some insight into five ways a banking relationship can help to grow the small business that you may not know.

1. Manage cash flow better.

Small business owners often wait to call their banker until they have a cash flow challenge. From examining accounts receivables and payables to find ways to get paid faster to identifying tools and strategies to manage seasonal or other irregular cash flow, she and her team dive into the business and make their best recommendations for its success.

2. Streamline payroll and payments.

Using today's powerful digital and online platforms, small businesses can also work with their banks to automate functions like payroll and recurring payments to save time. With the boom in digital payroll solutions, small business owners can effectively manage the day-to-day cash flow and increase efficiency. Payroll tax services can handle the withholdings that can also be paid electronically.

Payroll services providers also handle tax withholdings and assist companies with state and federal law compliance.

3. Facilitate relationships.

Bankers know everyone. Regardless of the contact you need, your banker is sure to have a referral for you. As a small business owner, you will more than likely outsource things like marketing, accounting, etc. Having a good relationship with a banker could save you time, money, and the headache of a long vetting process in the search for the right fit for your company. You may also consider contacting your banker for referral for internal partners like HR, attorneys, vendors or suppliers, etc.

4. Align your banking and tax goals.

Do not let your tax minimization strategy inadvertently undermine your banking needs. Have a meeting with your banker, attorney, and accountant to discuss tax and business strategy to get the best fit for your business. During this meeting, you should review your goals and objectives to create the best possible outcomes.

5. Work as your knowledgeable advisor.

Meet with your banker at least annually to discuss your plans for growth. Request that they perform an annual account review in which it evaluates the business's expenditures and identifies ways to save money. Your business banker should be responsive and available whether you have a quick question or need a strategic session. A good business banker can help you identify and pursue important growth opportunities.

ACCOUNTANT

When bringing aboard a Certified Public Accountant (CPA), you have to treat it like an interview for any position on your executive team. Namely, you want to know that the "candidate" has experience in your industry and whether they are the right fit to meet the goals and objectives for your brand. Here are some of the basic "interview questions" and key considerations when choosing a CPA.

Does This CPA Service Clients In My Industry?

It is it crucial that the CPA you are hiring has experience in YOUR industry. There are nuances across industries of which a general accountant or even a CPA may not be aware if they are not familiar with the requirement in your industry. In addition to industry-specific experience, you want to make sure they have experience with tax planning, tax forecasting, and tax preparation for your particular industry. This could make or break the success of your venture. Here are some great tips from Forbes, "Make sure the accountant you hire has other clients in the market you're in. Many industries are unique in terms of the best ways to track and optimize inventory, costs, or company expenses. An experienced CPA will help you navigate these areas efficiently and profitably."

Who Will Be Directly Handling My Account?

Since the CPA will be a critical part of the team, you want to make sure you know exactly who is handling your account when hiring an external partner. During your interview with the prospect, make sure to ask to meet the specific person who is handling your account. Remember, this is like any other candidate interview and you want to make sure you are comfortable with the selection process.

Some major considerations include:

- How accessible will the CPA be to you when you need them?
- Will it be easy to contact them when you have questions, need financial advice, or have a present crisis happening in your office?

Does This Firm Have the Capacity to Handle My Account?

Firm size and service are additional critical pieces to the BAIL

Team puzzle. Typically the larger the firm the less connected and personalized services you should expect. Conversely, a very small firm may not have the means or capacity to handle the range of services your business needs. For example, many CPA firms' services range from bookkeeping, tax preparation, and general accounting services. While others also provide financial planning, tax representation, audits and business consulting. If you need a company that performs audits or business valuations, make sure that's part of your criteria when seeking out a service provider.

How Can This CPA Help My Specific Business?

With regard to taxes due and general accounting and bookkeeping methods, there are lots of generalized methods in the marketplace. However, there are some industry nuances that your CPA should know to make sure you are gaining advantages and avoiding pitfalls with your taxes. For example, the cannabis and cryptocurrency industries have lots of nuances that can create a tax nightmare for a brand who are not well versed in the ever-changing tax regulations regarding those industries.

What Other Services Does The CPA Offer?

Having access to a full suite of services will provide useful for you in your business. Besides tax planning and preparation, services such as bookkeeping, financial planning, business consulting, audits, business valuations are great for businesses seeking to grow. You want to inquire about other services your CPA can provide and how those services can improve your business bottom line. You also want to ask about asset protection options or alternatives to shelter income and assets from lawsuits or other judgments.

Where Is The Best CPA For Me Located?

You do not have to be limited to your local area for a good CPA. With technology, geography is no longer an obstacle to connecting with the right professional. The market place is global, even with a brick and mortar local business. Busy professionals and business owners invite more efficient ways to get things done and they are open to things like video conferencing or teleconference calls with a trusted professional. If you are not restricted to state-specific advice, your CPA can be anywhere.

What Services Do I Need From The CPA?

Before you start this journey, you need to be crystal clear on the services you are seeking from your CPA. It can range from simple tax return preparation or as complicated as a multi-year tax plan or estate plan. When you establish your essential needs then you can use those as a starting point for the vetting process. After that, you can go through the interview process because you have made a preliminary determination that the CPA provides the services in which you are in need.

How Has The CPA Worked With And Benefited Business Owners Like Me?

Ask for references. Remember, this is like any other candidate interview. As a business owner, you must be results driven.

They should be willing to provide you with present or former client references. Make sure that you contact them to ask some key questions like services provided, response times, client contact/customer services, technology access, and whether they have seen turnover within the CPA firm. *Why would you want to know about turnover?* Because you want to be able to gauge whether your account will be moved from person to person due to high turnover rates.

What have they done for other businesses like yours? Ask for examples and outcomes. Then listen to what they say. From their answers, you can determine:

- Whether they are a good fit for your company,
- Whether your business can achieve a similar benefit, and
- How the relationship flow will work based on their past performance.

Focus on results, not generalizations. You do not have to be in this alone. Ask other business owners for referrals. Also, check online reviews and state licensing boards for any complaints or discrepancies in what they mentioned in their interview and what the digital footprint provides.

Verify, verify, verify. Your CPA may have the requisite industry knowledge, but you want to verify the number of years of experience the person who will be handling your company has in the industry. Even if the first person you connect with has everything on your checklist, interview two or three additional practitioners to have a well-rounded view of what is being offered.

At all costs, do not base your final decision strictly on pricing alone. Although pricing can be a major consideration, deciding factors should include how closely aligned is the practitioner with your companies value system. You can always choose to supplement your CPA services with other professionals like a bookkeeper, payroll processor, or even tax preparation services. This could help to keep costs low and maximize profits in the long run. Regardless of which option you choose, have a CPA that is the right fit aligned with your company.

HOW TO STOP BRAND STEALING THIEVES

INSURANCE PROFESSIONAL

Regardless of the type of business whether product or service based, you need to have insurance. Most people think that ANY insurance professional can properly advise you on the type of insurance that you need, but unfortunately, that is not the case. Your insurance professional needs to be versed in your industry and understand the unique needs of the industry to better suggest coverage options that you may not know about. However, there are ten insurance policy coverages that every business owners should consider:

1. General Liability Insurance

2. Property Insurance

3. Business owner's policy (BOP)

4. Commercial Auto Insurance

5. Worker's Compensation

6. Professional Liability Insurance, also known as Errors and Omissions Insurance.

7. Directors and Officers Insurance.

8. Data Breach.

9. Life Insurance.

10. Personal Umbrella Insurance.

The scope of this book does not lend for a full discussion of each one; however, we will discuss the pertinent ones below. Regardless of the type of business whether product or service based, you need to have insurance. Do not think that ANY insurance professional can properly advise you on the type of insurance that you need, but unfortunately, that is not the case. Your insurance professional needs to be versed in your industry and understand the unique needs of the industry to better suggest coverage options that you may not know about.

However, there are certain insurance policy coverages that every business owners should consider:

- General Liability Insurance is a product that every business owner needs to secure general liability insurance, even if it is a home-based business. This applies to home-based businesses as well. Generally, there are limitations on what a home-based business owner can recover under their homeowner's insurance policy. This type of policy protects your company against third-party claims for injuries.

- Business owner's policy (BOP) is a comprehensive package that outlines a suite of coverages a business would need. It typically provides cost savings due to the bundled services, like business property insurance, business interruption insurance, liability coverage, etc.

- Professional Liability Insurance, also known as Errors and Omissions Insurance. The policy provides defense and damages for failure to or improperly rendering professional services. You must have a separate policy for this coverage. These coverages are applicable to any service-based business including but not limited to, lawyers, accountants, consultants, notaries, real estate agents, insurance agents, hair salons, security professionals, and technology providers to name a few.

- Directors and Officers Insurance protects organizational leadership for claims against actions taken that affect the profitability or operations of the company. If a director or officer of your company, as a direct result of their actions on the job, finds him or herself in a legal situation, this type of insurance can cover costs or damages lost as a result of a lawsuit.

- Personal Liability insurance is about financial protection for you and your family. Most carry personal liability coverage as part of their homeowner's policy; however, I always suggest that business owners carry what is commonly called an Umbrella policy. The Umbrella policy is a personal liability policy that picks up where other policy limitations stop. For example, with auto insurance, there are policy limitations to the coverage. If there were a catastrophic injury that you cause to a third party, you would be personally liable for those injuries. Having an umbrella policy provides coverage where your present coverage stops.

There are several life insurance products that are recommended for business owners. The top products that I recommend are key man insurance and buy-sell agreement insurance.

- Key man insurance is life and disability insurance that provides coverage for key employees essential to the success of the company. The policyholder is the business; the business pays the premiums, and receives the payout if a covered event happens to the insured party, i.e., the key man.
- A buy-sell agreement is a legally binding agreement between co-owners of a business that determines the terms of what happens if a co-owner dies, is forced to leave the business or chooses to lease the business. There is an insurance product available to fund these types of agreements.

LAWYER

Before you make any major moves, start with connecting with a lawyer and an accountant. I have already discussed what the accountant does and the steps you need to go through to make the right choice. Frankly, It is somewhat obvious what the accountant can do for you and the need for one. Hiring an attorney is another matter altogether. Good business attorneys listen to your vision and assist you with the steps you need to take to create a legally sound entity, protect your personal and intellectual property while creating a growth positioned company. Attorneys can assist you with zoning, licensing, intellectual property, incorporating your business and creating a liability protection plan. Sounds great right?

Just like with accountants there are some general guidelines for dealing with lawyers. *Do not wait until you have a lawsuit to hire a lawyer.* Meaning if you have been served with a court summons…it is too late to be proactive. The time to engage an attorney is at the outset to get the proper guidance up front. *It is cheaper to be proactive than to be reactive.*

HOW TO STOP BRAND STEALING THIEVES

Here's the play when considering what type of attorney or firm meets your needs:

What's the right sized firm for your brand? Larger law firms usually mean larger bills. Most large law firms tend to charge hourly rates versus flat rates and for the entrepreneur that could break the bank. **CAUTION:** Do not make your counsel decision strictly on fees. There are numerous advantages of large firms versus smaller firms. To remain relevant, lawyers have had to specialize in practical areas especially solo practitioners. If you are going to opt for a smaller firm, make sure that the attorneys have the skills necessary to help you grow your business.

Types of Attorneys

Just like to you target doctors because of their unique specialty and skill set, with the specialization of lawyers you have to do the same. As a growth-minded entrepreneur, you want to target attorneys with specialized experience in the following areas:

Contracts. Seek out a lawyer who can handle the contracts that you will need for clients, customers, independent contractors, vendors, suppliers, etc. It is important that your attorney be capable of assisting you in responding to contracts that are presented to you from others.

Business organizations. What's the best business structure for your company? Your lawyer should know. You want to locate a lawyer who can help you understand the pros and cons of the various business organizational structures. Moreover, you want to have an attorney who can properly advise you on which structure is the best fit for your short and long term goals.

Real estate. If you have or are seeking to have a brick and mortar location, your attorney will need to have experience in real estate transactions. Whether you are leasing, buying, or utilizing shared space, there are contracts associated with your use or acquisition of the property. Most of the contracts are drafted in favor of the owner, but you can always negotiate based on the needs of your company. For example, for those that are renting, you want to always have a tenant's addendum that takes your needs into account. This will ensure that you receive the best treatment if there is a conflict.

Taxes and licenses. Most registration services are online now, but your lawyer should be responsible for filing your organizational documents, they can assist with filing your federal and state tax identification number and assist you with obtaining the proper licensing for the business.

Intellectual property. Intellectual property is somewhat of a specialized area and having access to an attorney with intellectual property expertise is crucial for any business entity, but especially for creative. There is more dedicated to intellectual property later in this book, but ask your potential lawyer during the interview process about their experience with intellectual property.

Data and Privacy. The best resource for assisting business owners with data privacy compliance education is the Federal

Communications Commission (FCC) (www.fcc.gov). The FCC provides a useful handout entitled, *"Ten Cybersecurity Tips for Small Businesses"*. You can also find it in the *How to Stop Brand Stealing Thieves Companion Toolkit*. There is also a useful tool called the Cyber-planner that assists in creating cyber plans for business owners. The FCC recommends the following steps for cybersecurity planning:

1. **Train employees in security principles.** This means establishing strong passwords, creating Internet policies, etc.

2. **Protect information, computers, and networks from cyber attacks.** Make sure you have updated virus protection, create a strong password policy, etc.

3. **Provide firewall security for your Internet connection.** Limit access to information to a

private network and make sure to have the best option for employees that work remotely.

4. **Create a mobile device action plan.** Mobile devices are susceptible to breach because of the cloud and other information sharing features.

5. **Make sure you have backup copies of important business data and information.** Regularly back up your critical data, including word processing documents, client information and more.

6. **Control physical access to computers and create user accounts for each employee**.

7. **Secure your Wi-Fi networks.** Restrict broadcasting your Service Set Identifier (SSID).

8. **Employ best practices on payment cards.** Work with banks and other payment processors to implement anti-fraud strategies at your company.

9. **Limit employee access to data and information and limit their ability to install the software.**

10. **Passwords and authentication.** Require employees to use a password to access information. Make sure these passwords have a high difficulty level to diminish the chance of outside compromise.

What to Ask Your Prospective Attorney?

You are in control of your brand and it is your responsibility to properly vet every prospective practitioner, including attorneys. Similar to the information you want to obtain from the accountant, you need to ascertain the lawyers experience with your industry. Never be afraid to ask flat out, **"Are you experienced?"** and then based on the answer, you will need to further inquire.

Your business attorney should operate much like those diagnostic machines used at the auto body shops. You should be able to "drive in" your business, present the facts, and your lawyer should be able to diagnose the problem and determine what needs to be done. For example, you have created a revolutionary product and want to take it to market. Your lawyer should quickly access that you will need a provisional patent at a minimum and a full patent at maximum. If your attorney does not specialize in the area, they should be connected to a ready resource that does. You should not be placed in a position to find a new lawyer for every specific legal problem that you have. Ask your attorney, **"How vast is your network? Just in case I need services outside of your direct expertise."**

Like with the CPA, **do they have other clients in your industry?** There should be baseline knowledge of the industry and what's happening in the industry. **If they do not have the baseline knowledge, are they willing to get up to speed?** Do your due diligence, you should see what types of organizations they are connected with, what type of information is in the waiting area, or on their website. A major reason you want to know if they represent anyone in your industry is that you want to make sure that you are not sitting in your competitor's attorney's office. You could run the risk of them using information obtained during your meeting to help your competition.

How do they communicate? Did you feel they were able to educate you on the market and explain the legal environment in a way that you could "get it"? Did they tell you what the law says and how that affects your business? Does this seem like a person that can teach and train your staff in this area? Do they have a blog or newsletter highlighting recent developments or providing information to help you in your business?

Who exactly will be working with my business? I was recently exposed to the finder, minder, or grinder concept for lawyers and it truly puts your abilities in perspective. The concept explains the three types of lawyers (and honestly, three types of business owners). "The "finder" scouts for business and brings in new clients; the "minder" takes on new clients and makes sure existing ones are happy; the "grinder" does the clients' work." The attorney working directly with your business should be a minder/grinder combination. The reason being is you want to know you are working with someone who is paying close attention to the details of your business and doing the work. **You must as the question, "Will you be doing the work or will that be someone else in your firm?"** If they are not the one doing the actual work, ask to meet with the person who is doing it. You must be comfortable with that person.

Ask, **"What is your billing policy?"** "Are you flexible in your billing?" Let me be clear, lawyers come in droves, right? You will read lots of Internet blogs that say, lawyers need to be completely flexible because there are so many. **Here is where you must be very careful with the play.** There may be droves of lawyers and DIY legal this or that; but, understand that you get what you pay for. It is important to do your due diligence upfront. There are lots of services that are provided for no to low cost.

There are different types of fee structures for legal services. Protecting your brand is really an investment in your legacy and your personal future, but there are limits to what you can handle from a fee standpoint.

Here's the play when you have a great match but they are outside of your budget: if you discover an attorney you want to work with your brand and you find out that you cannot afford the actual fees, ask, what services can/would you provide for my budget of X? This gives you the option of working with an attorney of choice and at your price. You can always build up to full service once your profits increase. You might also ask whether there is a payment plan and if so, what are the terms and conditions?

Fees: Flat Rates and Value-Based Pricing

In recent years, many lawyers, including myself, have opted to employ flat rate and value-based pricing models. Flat rate models are a one time charge for certain routine matters and may or may not include any out of pocket expenses. The flat rate model has been well received because the clients are clear on the total payment amount for the rendered services. When engaging multiple services on a flat rate billing model, make sure you are clear on deliverables, the scope of services, and payment terms so that you are not blindsided by fees that you thought were included in the flat rate pricing.

Most importantly, you want to be sure that you are clear on when the fees have to be paid and when services will be rendered. For example, we offer payment plans on most of our flat rate billing services; however, we do not deliver the product until full payment is rendered. Additionally, if there is a default on the flat rate payment plan, our office defaults to an hourly rate to account for services rendered up to and until the default payment. Any excess is returned to the client and we terminate the relationship for default.

Most attorneys, including our office, do not use the flat rate billing for litigation and negotiation matters. Why? The other side is highly unpredictable and it is always unclear how much "work" the other side will be in a given matter. It is difficult to estimate the time value of the representation in these matters. Also, there are certain layers and stages to litigation, which means that you have to account for any contingencies at each level. This makes it very difficult to create a flat rate charge that would be ample compensation if the matter goes left.

Regardless of the fee arrangement, you need to have this information in a written format.

Value-based billing is where the fees are based on the value of the cost savings. Value-based billing is similar to contingency in that it is derived from the perceived outcome of the case. For example, if a business owner is about to enter into a contractual arrangement that would be to his/her detriment, the attorney may base the fees on the amount of savings the client may receive from services rendered. If you are given a value based fee proposal, make sure that you fully understand the pricing model. Remember, the fees are not based on time spent, but oftentimes on amount of savings and complexity. There are mixed reviews about this pricing structure, however, it can be very good for the clients with lots at stake.

Retainer Fees

Most often retainer agreements are used as deposits for payments against future hourly fees. This is "unearned income" meaning that it is prepayment for future services rendered. If you are asked to pay a retainer, you want to know how the money will be used and that it will not go into the escrow abyss. You also want to make sure that your retainer agreement provides that any unused/unearned portions will be returned to you. Beware of lawyers who request an equity stake (ownership interest) in your business in lieu of fees.

Cost-Saving Strategies

When most people think of hiring a lawyer, they are paralyzed with fear of high fees, little work, and not having enough capital to cover the fees. Let us face it, lawyers are expensive, but there are several ways to keep costs low. Here's the play, start with understanding the right billing structure for you and your budget. Here's some useful information:

Hourly or per Diem rate. Billing by the hour or by the day.

Flat fee. An all-encompassing total fee for services.

Monthly retainer or package pricing: A monthly fee that entitles you to all the routine legal advice you need.

Contingent fee. Lawyers pay the upfront costs of the case in exchange for a percentage of the fees that are collected, plus reimbursement for expenses. Be comfortable bringing up a different payment method if the one they are proposing does not work for you. Oftentimes, attorneys will be flexible with fees under certain circumstances.

Entrepreneur Magazine gives some awesome tips on cost-saving strategies when dealing with attorneys. "No matter what type of billing method your attorney uses."

Here are some steps you can take to control legal costs:

- *Have the attorney estimate the cost of each matter in writing, so you can decide whether it is worth pursuing.* If the bill comes in over the estimate, ask why. Some attorneys also offer "caps," guaranteeing in writing the maximum cost of a particular service. This helps you budget and gives you more certainty than just getting an estimate.
- *Learn what increments of time the firm uses to calculate its bill.* Attorneys keep track of their time in increments as short as six minutes or as long as half an hour. Will a five-minute phone call cost you $50?

- *Request monthly, itemized bills.* Ask for monthly invoices, and review them. The most obvious red flag is excessive fees; this means too many people--or the wrong people--are working on your file. It is also possible you may be mistakenly billed for work done for another client, so review your invoices carefully.

- *See if you can negotiate prompt-payment discounts.* Request that your bill be discounted if you pay within 30 days of your invoice date. A 5-percent discount on legal fees can add thousands of dollars to your yearly bottom line.

- *Be prepared.* Before you meet with or call your lawyer, have the necessary documents with you and know exactly what you want to discuss. Fax needed documents ahead of time so your attorney doesn't have to read them during the conference and can instead get right down to business. And refrain from calling your attorney 100 times a day.

- *Meet with your lawyer regularly.* At first glance, this may not seem like a good way to keep costs down, but you'll be amazed at how much it reduces the endless rounds of phone tag that plague busy entrepreneurs and attorneys."–Cliff Ennico (www.entrepreneur.com/article/58326)

- You are in the position of power in your brand.

Your BAIL Team members work for you and should always work for the best interest of the company. Always ask questions until you have a clear understanding of your legal and financial pictures.

You have reached out to the banker, CPA, lawyer, and insurance professional.

Reflections: In the companion workbook, detail your experience with each one and examine the following:

Did you follow the suggested question pattern? If so, how did it help with your discussion?

If not, why not?

What went well with the discussion?

What did not go well with the discussion?

How or what will you adjust for the next discussion?

What are the top three critical steps that you will take to secure professional services you will need in the short term? Long term?

1. _____

_____

_____

2. _____

_____

_____

HOW TO STOP BRAND STEALING THIEVES

3. _____

_____

_____

3

INTELLECTUAL PROPERTY: THE MOST NEGLECTED REAL ESTATE

Most people do not realize that intellectual property is property, just like real estate, stocks, mutual funds, bonds, and personal property. My theory is that it is because it is intangible and some fail to see the value in our brainpower. Intellectual property is the only property that is purely, and uniquely yours from its inception. *Think about that.* Your concept, your business, your machine, etc., was given to you without effort and belongs only to you...protect it.

TRADEMARKS

Black's Law Dictionary defines a trademark as follows, "A distinctive mark, motto, device, or emblem, which a manufacturer stamps, prints, or otherwise affixed to the goods he produces, so that they may be identified in the market, and their origin be vouched for." Trademarks can be registered with the state and/or the United States. I always recommend that you file a federal trademark because it is valid in every US state and territory. While a state trademark limits your exclusive rights to that particular state.

For a federal trademark to be official, it must be registered with the United States Patent and Trademark Office (USPTO). Once registered with the USPTO the federal trademark is good for 10 years, with 10-year renewal terms. The USPTO required that between years five and six after registration that the registrant (that's you) must file an affidavit stating that the mark is still in use. If you fail to file the affidavit then your registration is canceled.

The first thing that you need to know is whether the trademark you want is available. Remember all trademarks are not registered and because they are not registered that doesn't mean that you can have them, it comes down to the owner's intent in the marketplace. There is something called a common law trademark and a registered trademark. The common law trademark, in essence, is an unregistered trademark that the owner places the marketplace on notice of their intent to take ownership in the mark. They do this by listing a ™ beside the mark or phrase, but they do not register the mark with the USPTO. This is why you must understand how to conduct a common law trademark search in addition to a formal trademark search.

A great starting point is to obtain a Trademark Research Report. This will allow you to see if the trademark is available before you attempt to register it. Trademarks are not free and the Trademark Research Report is not free, but it is money well spent. When you attempt to register a trademark by filing an application, the fee you pay is nonrefundable. The filing fees alone start around $325.00, and you do not want to get caught in a non-refundable fee situation multiple times.

This boils down to doing your due diligence. You want a properly conducted research report and you want to ask your proposed counsel whether they will be conducting that research report as part of the fee they have quoted.

This report is crucial because if someone else is already using the same or similar mark in the marketplace, you may actually be infringing on his or her intellectual property. If you are found to have been infringing on another company's brand. It will also help you make sure that you're not adopting or beginning to use somebody else's trademark because if it does, you could then be forced to give up your trademark.

As a caution, be very wary of these free trademark searches.

I've had people tell me, "Well LeTonya, I have already looked it up, I looked it up. I went through the trademark search and it is not there, nobody's using it." Only to find out that the free trademark search does not adequately check for common law trademarks.

No one can guarantee that your trademark would be approved, not even an attorney. The best course of action is to do your own due diligence, check the research, and get a consult from a trained intellectual property lawyer before paying out any money. Why? If something goes wrong you will have recourse through their errors and omissions policy. Which is a policy established to protct clients against mistakes and negligence of a licensed professional, like an attorney.

There are a lot of nuances and issues that come into play when you're looking at doing your trademark. Once you have registered your trademark, or for those who are seeking to stay with a common law trademark, you need to have a trademark watchdog. Your trademark watchdog is responsible for monitoring the marketplace trolling for infringers. For those that cannot afford an actual watchdog service, you can always set up a Google Alert. This will allow you to see who is using your name or slogan online. For picture marks, you can do a Google search for the picture and see where it is being used. This is by no means a catchall, but it is a simple system that you can put into place that will aid you in protecting your brand.

To infringe, the thief does not have to use the exact same mark. Quite frankly, most do not. It can just be something that is so similar that people may confuse it with your brand or product. This is not the same as having a similar product or service. This is a company in a similar industry that creates a similar logo, brand colors, or they are using slightly different terminology. They are borrowing from your credibility by confusing the consumer into believing that their brand is actually your brand. In order to have a viable infringement claim, you must be monitoring the mark. Think of it like squatters rights. If you are not utilizing the property and someone else openly does for a certain period of time, you run the risk of losing your ownership interest.

When you have done all of this, you want to be vigilant about enforcing your trademark. Once you are on notice that someone is potentially using your brand to build theirs, the first course of action is to reach out to the company and inform them you are placing them on notice of your concerns. Once the infringement is discovered you must act quickly because if you do not, in some places it can be considered a waiver.

When you reach out to make sure that you do it in writing. I can be in the form of a general letter or a cease and desist letter. This can get very tricky if they have been operating under a name or using a similar logo and have some independent notoriety. Let us say a competitor registered a domain that's similar to your trademark. Now a domain name dispute maybe your brand name is not so unique after all. If they're simply using a trademark on their website and It is similar to yours, you can send them a cease and desist letter. The best move is to try an amicably resolve the issue prior to filing a court claim.

If you make contact and they respond letting you know that they believe they are entitled to the mark and/or have a filing pending, you want to take necessary steps to file an opposition to that registration. This is why consulting an attorney or trademark expert is the best course of action. In the world of DIY everything, it is easy to think you do not need a lawyer for something like a filing. There are lots of things you do not necessarily need to spend money on but a trademark is not one of them.

COPYRIGHTS

Black's Law Dictionary defines copyright as a right granted by statute to the author or originator of certain literary or artistic productions, whereby he is invested, for a limited period, with the sole and exclusive privilege of multiplying copies of the same and publishing and selling them.

A copyright is the exclusive legal right, given to and originated to use, designate the use or designate to use to print publish perform, film record, etc. or distribute works the author or creator originated. The copyright protects intellectual property, authors, training and webinars that material is eligible for copyright protection.

Here's the play for copyright. Before you distribute your works, make sure that you include a © Copyright (Year) as part of the presentation, preferably in the footer of each presentation page. When presenting training or webinars, I dedicate an entire slide to the copyright notice. Depending on how young you are, you remember when watching VHS videos there was a copyright notice before the beginning of the movie.

HOW TO STOP BRAND STEALING THIEVES

Protect your property at the moment of birth. I liken it to having a child. When that child enters the world, you need to make sure that you obtain life insurance, even on the newborn. Copyrights are the same. When you go to do speaking engagements and you prepare your presentation, whether it is just a speech, whether it is off-the-cuff that is still your intellectual property. If you make an off-the-cuff comment, it's protected because it is part of the whole presentation. By placing the notice at the beginning of your presentation it is clear that you intend to protect everything that comest hereafter.

When you are booked for engagements where you will be providing your intellectual property ALWAYS inquire whether the presentations are going to be videotaped. If the answer is yes, make sure that you know how the footage will be later distributed, whether they will charge for the subsequent viewing and whether you will get a copy of the final version of the footage. There are lots of questions surrounding this that can be asked, but it is beyond the topics of this playbook.

Copyrights and trademarks are often confused. In addition, there are things that are not eligible for copyright. Information readily available in the public domain is not protected, facts, ideas, systems, methods of operations, etc. There are also times where you may have created a work that is not eligible for copyright because it derived from someone else's work.

How is a copyright created? Copyrights derive from an originator and for years the court was split as to exactly when a copyright ownership interest was developed. Prior to 2019, a copyright was considered protected at the time of inception, dissemination, and/or application. Previously, copyright did not have to be registered, to be a protected work.

Do you have to register it to be protected? Yes. In 2019, the Supreme Court has cleared up the split among the circuits and determined that rights attach at the moment copyright applications are accepted by the Copyright Office. When you put something out that you want to stake a copyright claim in, you must place the market on notice. You need to place a designation showing intent to copyright the material. You have effectively placed the marketplace on notice that there is intent to protect this item. *How does one do that?* By inserting a general copyright notice/symbol within the text. I am saying technically because if someone steals your stuff and they go ahead and they use it if you want to sue them in court you must have registered copyright first. You want to register your work so that if someone takes your idea and they profit from it you have a legal basis to sue for a share of the profits, or even prevent them from continuing to utilize the material for further gain. Now, we have to address the elephant in the room...what's that? The poor man's copyright.

POOR MAN'S COPYRIGHT

Poor man's copyright is a method of using registered dating by the postal service, a notary public or other highly trusted sources to date intellectual property, thereby helping to establish that the material has been in one's possession since a particular time. (Wikipedia). In layman's terms, you create something and take it to a notary or mail it to yourself registered or certified to show that you are the rightful owner. You keep the item sealed until you have to show the item to prove your claim.

Many of you will say getting a copyright is very expensive. It is actually less than what most Americans pay for one month of cellphone service. Once you register the copyright, now you have the legal title as the owner of the property. Due to the recent Supreme Court decision, you must be granted to copyright to even bring forth a court claim. If registration occurs within five years of creation it is considered what we call prima facie evidence. That means that you have met your burden of showing that you have an ownership right.

HOW TO STOP BRAND STEALING THIEVES

As the copyright holder, you have the authority to decide how and who can use the material. You can license the content or you can assign the ownership rights, etc. The copyright protects intellectual property. It used to be that copyrights were protected at the moment of creation right but it must be created in a fixed format quote-unquote "published", meaning it is outside of your brain in a tangible format. Unfortunately, that is no longer the case. If you want to protect your legal rights okay, meaning that you want to be able to sue people if they steal it, use it, profit from it, it must be registered. For more information about the copyright registration process, visit www.copyright.gov.

Here's the play:
What Intellectual Property protection does your company need? Trademark   Copyright   Other: _____

1. Did you decide to use a lawyer or an intellectual property service?

2. In the meantime, have you taken the steps to put the marketplace on notice of your intent to assert and ownership right into the product?

_____ inserted the TM symbol beside my trademark

_____ inserted the copyright symbol beside my creation

3. Whether you use a lawyer (which I highly recommend) or a trademark service, did you conduct your due diligence research?

4. If you opt to use a service versus a lawyer, did you read the fineprint and ask the same questions to properly vet their ability to assist you with your trademark?

5. If using a trademark service, what is your recourse if someone does not properly complete the work?

6. How will you recover if it is not properly completed and you do not have your trademark issued?

4

How to Successfully Barter & Collaborate

I N today's business climate, entrepreneurs need to be skilled at leveraging relationships to help their business grow and thrive. One of the ways that my personal brand grew was through barter and collaboration. Both have high risk and high rewards. In this chapter, you will learn some strategies to have a mutually advantageous barter and collaboration relationship.

Barter

I know, I just said the "B-word" right? I have heard time and time again about the bartering nightmares where you contact someone and you make an agreement to work together and it does not work out. The main reasons I have heard is, "I feel like I put more in to the deal than I got out of the deal" or "I did my part and he/she did not do their part", etc., etc., etc.

Let us start with some general considerations or questions you must answer before you even approach the company with which you want to barter:

1. **Is there a way to redirect your dollars or reposition money to pay for services, instead of bartering?** Some people start with bartering without first determining whether they have the funds to pay for services. Let us start there. Are there funds that can be temporarily redirected to pay for the services that you need? If the answer is yes, temporarily redirect the funds and pay for the services. This

means there are fewer areas in which you may need to barter your products or services, why? Keep in mind that any service or product that you barter must equate to an equal **value** exchange or one party will feel they have been slighted.

2. **Are YOU willing to put in the work that it is going to take for you to move your business to the next level?** How hard are you willing to work to make sure that your business grows? Oftentimes, the barter may be unnecessary because you have the requisite skills, talent, and time to do the things that you are seeking to get through the barter. This may be for a temporary timeframe; but it is worth the effort if you can save yourself some headaches down the road.

3. **What products or services do you have to offer for the barter relationship?** Barter is not a negative thing, however when you are looking to barter you

may feel somewhat inferior because you may not have the funds to outright pay for the services. *Get over that right now!*

The bottom line is, you have to ask yourself, *"What value can I add?"* When you start from a value position versus a need-based position, you will see yourself with an advantage versus a detriment. Working from this vantage point, always approach your prospect from the position of what's in it for them. Once you answer that question for them, it puts you in a better bargaining position to then ask, now, what's in it for me? *Lead with value and close the deal.*

4. **What products or services do you need from the barter?** When you look at your network, how do you decide with whom you want to work? Do some research, study your network and see who is in it and

what they are offering. You can perform a Google search, you can see what they're working on, who they are connected with; you can go to their website, review their social media pages, etc., what do they have that you want? You can see what they are working on and determine what you have to offer in the value exchange and determine what you have anything of value to offer.

5. **What are you willing to sacrifice to make the barter a success?** As entrepreneurs you must ask yourself, what sacrifices am I willing to make? If you are not willing to make any sacrifices, it is going to be very difficult for you to get other people to make sacrifices to help your business grow.

Here is the Play:

Answer the previous five questions before you get there. Use the answers to those questions to formulate your pitch.

Why? This places you in a great negotiating position because you are coming to the table with an offer verses a request. What may surprise you is, that person may offer to simply pay you for the services. You want to make sure that you always approach people from a position of strength even if they do not need what you have to offer. They may know someone who does or the need may arise at a later time. If that happens you are top of mind.

Now, you have presented your value and they have accepted. *What was your negotiated exchange?* Here is where the rubber meets the road. Some people think just because money is not exchanging hands that you do not need a written agreement that is not the case. Remember, before paper money existed, the barter system was in place. Due to the fact there is a value exchange, deliverables, and expectations of performance, you want to make sure that you have your agreement encapsulated within a barter agreement.

What are the deliverables? What are the expectations?

The terms of the written barter agreement are driven by the value exchange, deliverables, and expectations. In addition to these, you have to determine the following:

4. Whether there is an exchange of confidential information and if so, how will you deal with that?

5. Will either party share, use, or create intellectual property? If so, how will you deal with these collectively and individually?

6. What happens if there is a dispute?

7. Which state law will govern the agreement if the parties are in different states?

8. What constitutes a default?

9. What's the recourse if one party defaults?

These are just some of the top questions that need to be

answered when entering into a barter arrangement. There is a sample barter agreement and barter agreement checklist available in the companion toolkit.

Collaboration

Collaborations and barters are two very different creatures. Barters are simply an exchange of products and services perceived as equally valuable to the parties. Collaboration is where two or more parties work together to produce or create something. It is crucial to understand the distinction because a failure to understand the distinction could result in your giving up a right or interest in a valuable commodity.

The pre-work of what to do before entering into a collaborative arrangement is the same to how you approach the decision about bartering, up and until a certain point. For collaborations, there are some upfront considerations that need to happen before you have the collaboration conversation. Before we jump into that discussion, I want to share some of the benefits of collaboration.

Collaboration allows you to leverage the skillset of others and take advantage of broader opportunities instantly. It can expand your reach exponentially without you having to do much more than agree to a working relationship and perform. It can also help you to secure projects that you would not otherwise be eligible for or equipped to handle. When deciding whether to collaborate, the crucial conversation starts with you, not the potential collaborator.

Am I ready to collaborate...with you?

The buck always starts and stops with you. Before you connect with another brand, have a fireside chat with yourself. Take a good look at your reputation in your industry.

Here's the play Fireside Chat: Are you ready?

1. What does the marketplace say about your brand?

2. How can your reputation impact the collaborator and the project?

3. What is your working style?

4. What is your value system?

5. Can you be trusted?

6. Are you capable and available to meet the demand?

7. What has been your past experience with other collaborations?

Here's the play after the Fireside Chat: After having the self-chat and conducting a critical review of your potential collaborator, answer the following:

1. What have you determined?

2. Is this the right fit?

3. Do you foresee this being a profitable venture for all parties involved?

You must conduct this critical analysis for each potential

collaborator.   After that, you can now focus on the collaboration.

Am I Ready for This Project?

Here's the play: Determine if there is a TRUE need for a collaborator to make the project a reality.   Once you answer yes, then you need to do the following:

1. Create a division of tasks, duties, and deliverables that includes quality, quantity, and due dates. Bottom line is, the who, what, how, where, and when questions will all need to be answered.

2. Discuss these thoroughly with your collaborator and be sure they understand the expectations set.

3. In addition to these, you have to discuss credit, ownership and any permissible use of private information.

The critical question for you is, "Are you ready? Is the project inside or outside of your comfort zone?" Once you determine that you are ready for the project, there are several essential agreements that you need to make sure that you have in place.

Here's the play: Get your agreements ready to present to the collaborator. First, make sure that you have a non-disclosure agreement available for them to sign, before you share any details. The non-disclosure agreement is a binding agreement between parties or entities where they agree not disclose information that may be exchanged between the parties that is confidential in nature and to treat specific information as a trade secret. It is also important that you include that any documents exchanged will be returned and that no copies shall be made of confidential documents provided.

With collaborations, like barters, if you are the person with the initial vision, you need to make sure that you have an upfront agreement. I suggest that clients obtain a non-circumvent agreement for collaborators. This would prevent the situation where you give the vision and you all start working on it. Then they end up taking it and doing the project; but they leave you out. Another contract you can use as well is a non-compete agreement. The non-compete agreement, or covenant not to compete, is an agreement under which one party agrees not to enter into or start a similar profession or trade, etc., in competition against another party. You can find a sample in the companion toolkit. After you have received the non-disclosure, then you can share your ideas and get to work. Be sure to remain in control of the flow of information. My suggestion is that you provide collaborators with information strictly on a need to know basis.

When you agree to enter into a barter relationship with someone, you want to make sure that you have a barter agreement in place. Like with collaborators, make sure you have the non-discosure agreements executed or you may opt to place a clause to that effect in your barter agreement. If you opt for inclusion only in the formal agreement, take care not to share any proprietary information with that is not protected. Unlike collaborators, the barter relationship is like any other contract, except instead of exchanging money you are exchanging goods and services.

The essential elements of the barter agreement is the same as any other contract except, the payment is based on providing a product or service *in exchange* for products or services.

Here's the play for barter agreements: It must include the terms and the conditions of the exchange. It is important to note details of how you will handle intellectual property ownership, usage, licensing, etc. It should include provisions to handle default or failure to perform, what is the recourse that the parties have if the other party defaults. Additionally, barter agreements typically include the market value of the products or services to be exchanged.

These are all essential contracts to make your barter or collaboration a successful venture. Best wishes and may you achieve global growth.

Top Essential Documents (These Samples & More included in our Companion Entrepreneurs Toolkit)

HOW TO STOP BRAND STEALING THIEVES

1.   Sample Articles of Incorporation

2.   Sample By-Laws

3.   Sample LLC Operating Agreement

4.   Barter Agreement

5.   Collaboration Agreement

6.   Work for Hire Agreement

7.   Non-Disclosure Agreement

8.   Non-Compete Agreement

9.   Independent Contractor Agreement

10. Confidentiality Agreement

11. Website Terms of Use

12. Photo-Video Release

13. Professional Services Contract (for service based

businesses)

14.   Sales Contract (for product based businesses)

15.   Letters of Intent

16.   Business Proposal

17.   Trademark Usage Authorization

18.   Copyright Usage Authorization

IMPORTANT   RESOURCES   FOR   EVERY
ENTREPRENEUR

Government Agencies

1.   US PATENT AND TRADEMARK OFFICE www.uspto.gov

2.   COPYRIGHT OFFICE www.copyright.gov

3.   SMALL BUSINESS ADMINISTRATION www.sba.gov

4.   INTERNAL REVENUE SERVICE www.irs.gov

GLOSSARY

Barters: an exchange of products and services perceived as equally valuable to the parties.

B.A.I.L.: Acronym for Banker, Accountant, Insurance Professional and Lawyer.

Barter Agreement: a formal agreement outlining the exchange of goods and/or services for goods and/or services.

Billing Policy: a written policy of how a company issues bills and requires payment.

Brainstorm Team: a group of individuals that come together to work through possibilities and strategies to develop options to meet a stated goal or objective.

Business owner's policy (BOP) is a comprehensive package that outlines a suite of coverage a business would need. It typically provides cost savings due to the bundled services, like business property insurance, business interruption insurance, liability coverage, etc.

Buy-sell Agreement: a legally binding agreement between co-owners of a business that determines the terms of what happens if a co-owner dies, is forced to leave the business or chooses to lease the business.

Collaboration: where two or more parties work together to produce or create something.

Collaborator: a person who works jointly with others on a project or activity until its completion.

Contract: a written or spoken agreement intended to be enforceable by law.

Copyright: a right granted by statute to the author or originator of certain literary or artistic productions, whereby he is invested, for a limited period, with the sole and exclusive privilege of multiplying copies of the same and publishing and selling them.

Copyright holder: legal owner of a copyright.

Cost saving strategies: plans or processes developed to reduce costs and save money.

Directors and Officers Insurance protects organizational leadership for claims against actions taken that affect the profitability or operations of the company. If a director or officer of your company, as a direct result of their actions on the job, finds him or herself in a legal situation, this type of insurance can cover costs or damages lost as a result of a lawsuit.

Due Diligence: reasonable steps taken by a person in order to satisfy a legal requirement, especially in buying or selling something.

Errors and Omissions (see professional liability)

Executed Agreement: the signing of a document signed by persons authorized to bind the party to the terms and condition of the agreement.

Fee Structure: is a chart or list highlighting the price points on

HOW TO STOP BRAND STEALING THIEVES

various business services or activities.

General Liability Insurance is a product that protects your company against third-party claims for injuries.

Intellectual Property: a work or invention that is the result of creativity, such as a manuscript or a design, to which one has rights and for which one may apply for a patent, copyright, trademark, etc.

Key Man Insurance: life and disability insurance that provides coverage for key employees essential to the success of the company. The policyholder is the business; the business pays the premiums, and receives the payout if a covered event happens to the insured party, i.e., the key man.

Mastermind group: is a group of two or more people coming together in harmony to solve problems.

Necessary success component: an element that is so ingrained in the success of the project that by not having it the project cannot succeed.

Need to know basis: a tight security method in which information is only given to those who can present a good case for knowing about a project.

Non-circumvent: It generally provides that each party shall use the other party's information only for the purpose of pursuing a business relationship between the parties. It protects the disclosing party against the other when the other tries to bypass the disclosing party and pursue the business opportunity.

Non-compete: an agreement, clause, or provision that restricts the parties from competing against each other in the same market.

Non-disclosure agreement: a binding agreement between parties or entities where they agree not disclose information that may be exchanged between the parties that is confidential in nature and to treat specific information as a trade secret.

Patent: a form of intellectual property that gives its owner the legal right to exclude others from making, using, selling, and importing an invention for a limited period of years, in exchange for publishing an enabling public disclosure of the invention.

Poor Man's Copyright: a method of using registered dating by the postal service, a notary public or other highly trusted sources to date intellectual property, thereby helping to establish that the material has been in one's possession since a particular time.

Pre-work: what to do before the start of something.

Professional Liability Insurance, also known as Errors and Omissions Insurance. The policy provides defense and damages for failure to or improperly rendering professional services. You must have a separate policy for this coverage. These coverages are applicable to any service-based business including but not limited to, lawyers, accountants, consultants, notaries, real estate agents, insurance agents, hair salons, security professionals, and technology providers to name a few.

Provider (Service Provider): an individual, company, or entity that provides an identified service.

Red Flag: a metaphor used to indicate a particular problem is at hand.

Signatory: a party that has signed an agreement.

Think Tank: the top-level squad that comes to the table bringing a necessary success component.

Trademark: A distinctive mark, motto, device, or emblem, which a manufacturer stamps, prints, or otherwise affixed to the goods he produces, so that they may be identified in the market, and their origin be vouched for.

Trademark Infringement: is the unauthorized use of a trademark or service mark on or in connection with goods and/or services in a manner that is likely to cause confusion, deception, or mistake about the source of the goods and/or services.

Trademark Watchdog: a monitor to potential infringement

ACKNOWLEDGMENTS

I want to first express my gratitude to God for imparting the wisdom and vision to create this book. It was what seemed like an impossible journey or ups and down, but I am grateful for my family who supports all of my wild endeavours, including writing this book. To my son, Charvez L. Moore, you are my greatest accomplishment and inspiration. Since you were a very small child, you have always pushed me, encouraged me, and made my life full of joy. Thanks to my mother, Patricia C. Moore who has burned up the road with me from one event to another, helping me to share words of encouragement and educational information with entrepreneurs throughout the country. To my father Albert G. Moore, who helped me to see that even people who have been in business for decades can still use what I have to offer. Thanks for always being proud of my many accomplishments both in life and in business. To my sister, Kathy L. Moore, thanks for continuing to support my dreams and standing in prayer for me, when I could not pray for myself. Thank you to my pastor, friend, and brother, Prophet Mario C. Brown, your wise counsel, spiritual insight and training has helped me to understand that this God given message is worthy of people listening. Thanks for being one of the first beta readers and giving your insight as a business professional and sharing your candid feedback, Dr. Nicholas Bolden, Andrea Ball, Dominique LaFrance. Thanks to my Kingdom Church (Auburn, AL) family for your many prayers and support.

Thanks to some of my Brand Protection Accelerator first cohort group, Renatta L. Fleming, Deborah Franklin, and Lakichay Nadirah Muhammad for encouraging me to FINISH THE BOOK and supporting the vision of the project by entrusting your brands with me. I am forever grateful to each of you and I am better since we have met.

SPECIAL OFFERS

Get the Workbook & Toolkit Bundle Now! Work through your plan before you work with your service providers and collaborators. Arm yourself with sample agreements to present and secure for your protections. Go to bit.ly/BSTBundleDeal Now!

WANT TO ATTEND LETONYA'S BUSINESS GROWTH INTENSIVE (a $2500 value) AT A FACTION OF THE COST? You got it! In appreciation for your support, LeTonya is sharing a secret link (just for you) to attend her Mastermind Intensive in select locations or virtually for a fraction of the cost. Visit bit.ly/BPAIntensive for your exclusive rate.

97

360° BRAND PROTECTION ACADEMY™

SAVE $2000.00 NOW!

The 360° Brand Protection Academy™ is a seven week legal and business education course designed to provide new and growth driven business owners with the necessary tools to legally prepare, protect and propel their budding brand.

The course faculty is comprised of lawyers, CPAs, insurance professionals, financial experts, and all essential professionals every entrepreneur needs; but cannot afford at one time. The course features live virtual training, on demand availability, one-on-one strategic planning, and more! In appreciation of your support in purchasing this book, you receive the secret link to save $2000.00! Reserve your slot in the 360° Brand Protection Academy™ TODAY (while supplies last)! Go to bit.ly/BPADeal Now!

CONNECT WITH LETONYA

Subscribe to the Podcast

https://www.spreaker.com/show/power-of-attorney

Also available on Anchor, Apple Podcasts, Soundcloud, Castbox and more.

Subscribe on YouTube

https://www.youtube.com/c/RealPerspectivesTV

Join the 360 Brand Protection Facebook Group

Follow the Hashtags

#BrandProtectionTip #youmightneedalawyerif

#globalbrandprotector

Watch on Amazon FireTV

https://www.amazon.com/Real-Perspectives-LeTonya-Moore-Esq/dp/B07MF43P82

LETONYA F. MOORE

#BrandProtectionTip

Have consultants and independent contractors sign appropriate Confidentiality and Invention Assignment Agreements

-THE GLOBAL BRAND PROTECTOR

WWW.IPROTECTYOURBRAND.COM

100

-#BRANDPROTECTIONTIP

Obtain trademark registrations for company products and services

-THE GLOBAL BRAND PROTECTOR

WWW.IPROTECTYOURBRAND.COM

-#BRANDPROTECTIONTIP

You can't copyright something you saw on someone else's post first...

-THE GLOBAL BRAND PROTECTOR

WWW.IPROTECTYOURBRAND.COM

-#BRANDPROTECTIONTIP

Make sure your company is not infringing the intellectual property rights of others

-THE GLOBAL BRAND PROTECTOR

WWW.IPROTECTYOURBRAND.COM

-#BRANDPROTECTIONTIP

Display the "TM" or "SM" or "®" notice displayed properly on all company literature

-THE GLOBAL BRAND PROTECTOR

WWW.IPROTECTYOURBRAND.COM

ABOUT THE AUTHOR

LeTonya F. Moore, JD is an American attorney-entrepreneur and media personality. She boasts almost 20 years of professional experience and has leveraged what she has learned to show others how to create a legacy and protect their brand. LeTonya is a fourth generation entrepreneur who is committed to breaking the cycle of failing to create and leave a viable business for her family.

After expanding her Brand Protection message to the UK, she has become affectionately known as the "Global Brand Protector™, a moniker which she wears proudly. Her personal goal is to assist global minded business owners with getting global ready by providing access to quality legal and brand protection services in a cost effective manner. In 2019, LeTonya launched **"What Other Lawyers Won't Tell You"**, a free legal education series providing information, education, and insight on topics and nuiances of legal topics near and dear to the hearts of the legacy driven entrepreneur. Find out more at bit.ly/WhatOthersWontTellYou.

LeTonya created the **360° Brand Protection Academy** developed to teach, train, and equip entrepreneurs and professionals with the essential success tools to protect, propel, and profit from their brand. There is an application required to receive an invitation to be a part of the academy which can be found at bit.ly/brandproacademy. LeTonya's desire is to pour all she has into creating success strategies to assist others in legacy creation for subsequent generations. LeTonya host a Mastermind Group and a weekend series where attendees leave with a blueprint to propel their business forward.

LeTonya is a recipient of the 2019 Enterprising Woman Award by Enterprising Woman Magazine, 2019 Celebrate A Sista Award, 2019 Real Chicks Rock Woman of the Year Award.

To learn more about LeTonya Moore visit her official website at www.iprotectyourbrand.com
Follow her on Facebook @iprotectyourbrand
Twitter @letonyamoore IG/letonyamoore
LinkedIn LeTonya Moore